THIS BOOK BELONGS TO...

Name: Age:

Favourite player:

2023/24

My Predictions **Actual**

Leeds United's final position:

Leeds United's top scorer:

Championship winners:

Championship top scorer:

FA Cup winners:

EFL Cup winners:

Contributors: Peter Rogers, Sam Tighe.

A TWOCAN PUBLICATION

978-1-915571-62-5

£10

PICTURE CREDITS: Leeds United Football Club, Action Images, Alamy and Press Association.

LUFC

CONTENTS

THE CHAMPIONSHIP SQUAD 2023/24

Illan MESLIER 1

POSITION: Goalkeeper COUNTRY: France DOB: 02/03/2000

Former France under-21 international goalkeeper Illan Meslier was ever-present in Leeds United's 2021/22 Premier League campaign.

The 23-year-old was once again installed as first choice 'keeper at Elland Road by new manager Daniel Farke ahead of the 2023/24 Championship campaign. The excellent French stopper is now in his fifth season with Leeds United having joined the club from Lorient in 2019.

Luke AYLING 2

POSITION: Defender COUNTRY: England DOB: 25/08/1991

Long-serving right-back Luke Ayling has amassed over 250 appearances in Leeds United colours since joining the club from Bristol City back in 2016.

A loyal Leeds United servant, the experienced defender has sampled highs and lows during his time at Elland Road, but remains a popular and much-valued member of the first-team squad. He netted his first goal of the 2023/24 season to ensure the Whites took a point from their Elland Road meeting with West Bromwich Albion in August 2023.

Junior **FIRPO** 3

POSITION: Defender **COUNTRY:** Spain **DOB:** 22/08/1996

Left-back Junior Firpo adds experience to Daniel Farke's defensive unit at the age of 27 and is now one of the senior players in the squad.

A former Spain under-21 international, Firpo has featured in over 40 Premier League fixtures following his 2021 transfer to West Yorkshire from Barcelona. The versatile defender added goals to his game too last season when he was on target in the FA Cup victory away to Accrington Stanley in January and the Premier League triumph over Southampton at Elland Road in February.

Ethan **AMPADU** 4

POSITION: Midfielder **COUNTRY:** Wales **DOB:** 14/09/2000

Defensive midfielder Ethan Ampadu agreed a four-year deal with Leeds United in July 2023 after the Whites lured the highly rated Wales international away from Chelsea.

A mobile and competitive midfielder, Ampadu will add steel to the Leeds midfield and provide a defensive shield in front of the defence. Ampadu impressed during his debut as the Whites kicked-off the 2023/23 campaign with a 2-2 draw against Cardiff City at Elland Road.

Charlie **CRESSWELL** 5

POSITION: **Defender** COUNTRY: **England** DOB: **17/08/2002**

A product of the Leeds United Academy, central defender Charlie Cresswell is highly regarded at Elland Road and agreed a new long-term contract with the club ahead of the 2023/24 Championship campaign.

The son of former Leeds striker Richard Cresswell, Charlie enjoyed an extremely beneficial Championship loan spell with Millwall last season. His experience gained from performing regularly at second tier level last season should stand him in great stead this season as Leeds look to bounce straight back to the Premier League.

Liam **COOPER** 6

POSITION: **Defender** COUNTRY: **Scotland** DOB: **30/08/1991**

The opening day of the 2023/24 season certainly proved to be an afternoon of mixed fortunes for captain Liam Cooper. The ever-reliable Scottish international took the mantle of scoring the first goal of the Daniel Farke era at Elland Road, but was later stretchered off with a foot injury which was expected to sideline him for around two months.

An extremely shrewd £600,000 signing from Chesterfield back in 2014, Cooper has legendary status at Elland Road having now made over 250 appearances at the heart of the Leeds United defence.

THE CHAMPIONSHIP SQUAD 2023/24

Joël **PIROE** 7

POSITION: Forward **COUNTRY:** Netherlands **DOB:** 02/08/1999

Leeds United boosted their firepower in August 2023 with the signing of Dutchman marksman Joël Piroe from Championship rivals Swansea City.

Over the previous two seasons, the former Netherlands under-20 international had fired home an incredible 41 goals in 88 Championship appearances for the Welsh club.

With fantastic movement across the frontline and a proven eye for goal, the 24-year-old striker will certainly be a key man in this new-look Daniel Farke side.

Glen **KAMARA** 8

POSITION: Midfielder **COUNTRY:** Finland **DOB:** 28/10/1995

Finnish international midfielder Glen Kamara joined Leeds United in August 2023 from Glasgow Rangers and agreed a four-year deal with the Whites.

A product of the Arsenal Academy, Kamara reached the Gunners' first team and was also loaned to Southend United and Colchester United during his time at the Emirates Stadium. He made great strides in Scotland after joining Dundee in the summer of 2017 and in January 2019 he was signed by Scottish giants Rangers. A Scottish Premier League title-winner at Ibrox in 2020/21, tough tackling Kamara is sure to bring real tenacity to Leeds' promotion push.

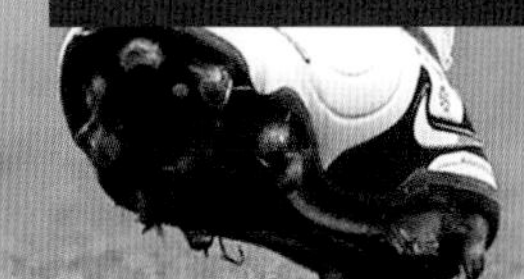

THE CHAMPIONSHIP SQUAD 2023/24

Patrick **BAMFORD** 9

POSITION: Forward **COUNTRY:** England **DOB:** 05/09/1993

Now with over half a century of goals for Leeds United to his name following a summer 2018 transfer from Middlesbrough, Patrick Bamford will be expected to be right amongst the goals again this season as Leeds bid to return to the Premier League.

With the ability to operate anywhere across the front line, Bamford's movement and finishing skills should make him one of the most feared strikers at Championship level in 2023/24.

Crysencio **SUMMERVILLE** 10

POSITION: Forward **COUNTRY:** Netherlands **DOB:** 30/10/2001

Goalscoring winger Crysencio Summerville netted Leeds' all-important late equaliser against Cardiff City on the opening weekend of the new season to ensure the Whites put a point on the board at the first time of asking.

A Dutch under-21 international, Summerville joined from Feyenoord in September 2020. He enjoyed a real breakthrough campaign last season and is sure to have a big part to play at Elland Road in 2023/24.

Jaidon **ANTHONY** 12

POSITION: Forward **COUNTRY:** England **DOB:** 01/12/1999

Jaidon Anthony completed a transfer deadline day move from AFC Bournemouth to Leeds United when he agreed a season-long loan at Elland Road for 2023/24.

Hackney-born Anthony began his youth career with Arsenal before joining the Cherries and progressing through the ranks on the South Coast. The skilful winger played a key role in Bournemouth's promotion from the Championship in 2021/22 and has also played over 30 times in the Premier League.

Kristoffer **KLAESSON** 13

POSITION: Goalkeeper **COUNTRY:** Norway **DOB:** 27/11/2000

An important member of the club's goalkeeping ranks, Norwegian under-21 international Kristopher Klaesson arrived at Elland Road in July 2021 from Valerenga.

After mainly featuring in the club's under-21 development side, Klaesson's first-team debut arrived in March 2022 when Illan Meslier was forced off injured in the Whites' Premier League match away to Wolverhampton Wanderers. It proved to be a memorable introduction to the first-team scene as Leeds stormed back from 2-0 down to edge a five-goal thriller 3-2.

Joe
RODON
14

POSITION: **Defender** COUNTRY: **Wales** DOB: **22/10/1997**

A full Wales international with over 35 full caps for his country, central defender Joe Rodon joined Leeds United in August 2023 on a season-long loan deal from Premier League Tottenham Hotspur.

The 6ft 4in defender began his career with Swansea City where rave reviews led to a reported £11m move to Spurs in October 2020. Widely recognised as a ball-playing centre-back, Rodon's skill set is sure to suit the style that Daniel Farke wishes to introduce at Elland Road this season.

Stuart
DALLAS
15

POSITION: **Defender** COUNTRY: **Northern Ireland** DOB: **19/04/1991**

All at Elland Road hope to see Northern Ireland international Stuart Dallas back in action for the Whites during the 2023/24 season.

A long-term injury prevented Dallas from featuring at all in the 2022/23 campaign and the Whites certainly missed his on-pitch versatility and commitment to the cause. With the experience of over 250 games for the club, the 32-year-old's return to action will be a huge boost to Leeds United.

THE CHAMPIONSHIP SQUAD 2023/24

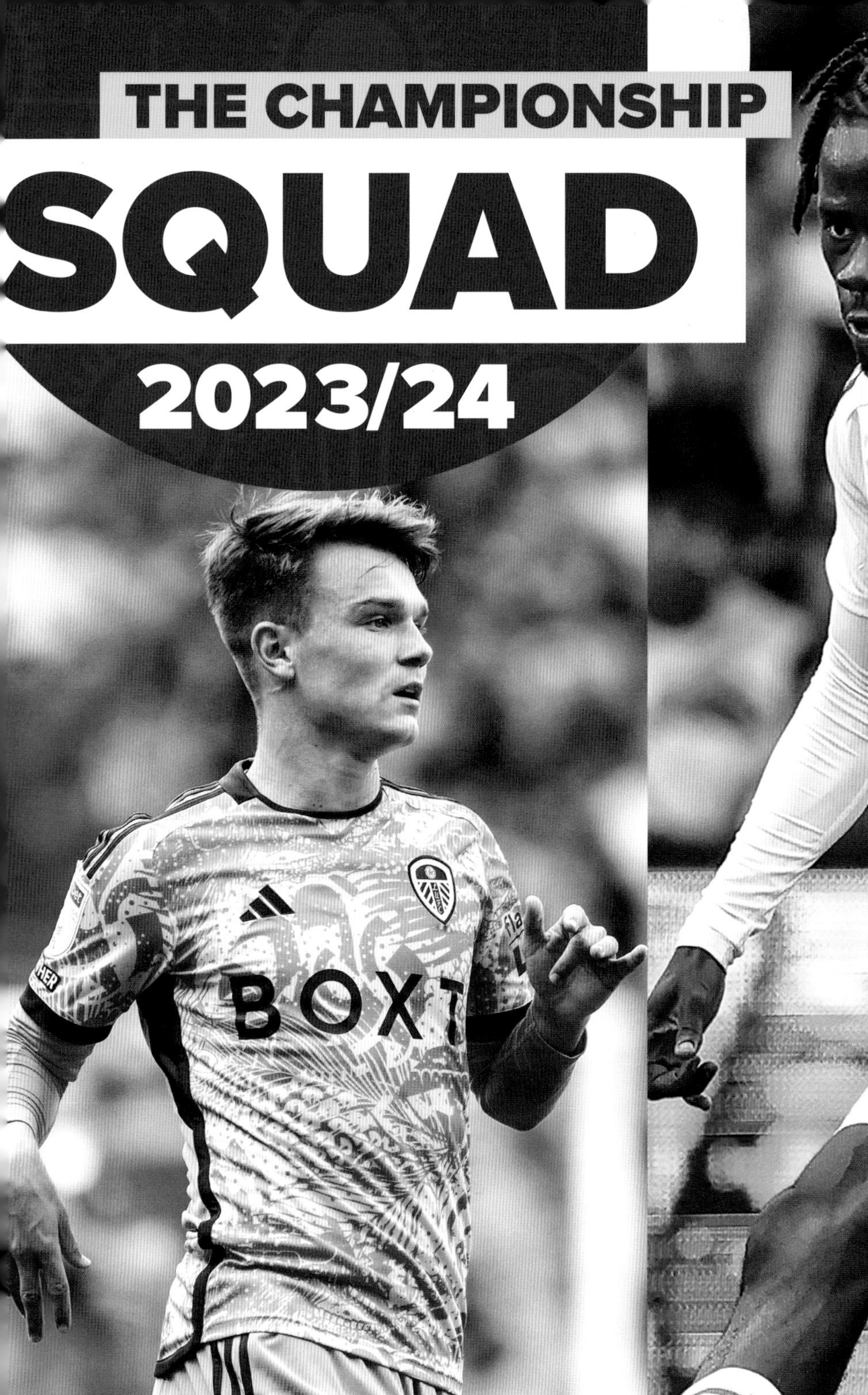

Jamie SHACKLETON 17

POSITION: Midfielder **COUNTRY:** England **DOB:** 08/10/1999

Jamie Shackleton is another product of the club's Academy system who began his association with the club as a seven-year-old.

Progressing through the age groups he made his first-team debut in a 4-1 victory over Derby County in August 2018.

Able to operate as a defensive midfielder or at right-back, Shackleton is closing in on 100 appearances for the Whites. Together with Leeds teammate Charlie Cresswell, Shackleton spent last season on loan with Millwall and be hoping that the Championship experience he gained at the Den will serve him well this season.

Darko GYABI 18

POSITION: Midfielder **COUNTRY:** England **DOB:** 18/02/2004

Darko Gyabi joined Leeds from Manchester City in July 2022. A central midfielder with all the attributes to enjoy a successful career in the game, Gyabi made his first-team debut for the Whites in the November 2022 EFL Cup tie away to Wolverhampton Wanderers.

He also tasted Premier League action for the first time when he made a substitute appearance against his former club at Elland Road on 28th December.

The 19-year-old also featured in this season's EFL Cup match with Shrewsbury Town.

Daniel
JAMES

20

POSITION: **Midfielder** COUNTRY: **Wales** DOB: **10/11/1997**

Wales winger Daniel James spent the majority of the 2022/23 season on loan with Fulham and also represented his county in the 2022 FIFA World Cup finals in Qatar.

Signed from rivals Manchester United in 2021, James' phenomenal speed makes him a true match-winner. After playing a big part in Leeds United's Premier League survival in 2021/22, supporters will be hoping his eye-catching performances can help create a successful 2023/24 campaign at Elland Road.

THE CHAMPIONSHIP SQUAD 2023/24

Pascal
STRUIJK
21

POSITION: Defender **COUNTRY:** Netherlands **DOB:** 11/08/1999

A regular face in the Leeds United team over the past three seasons, Dutch defender Pascal Struijk has been a highly consistent and reliable performer for the Whites.

With the flexibility to operate as a centre back or as a defensive midfielder, left-footed Struijk's presence always brings great balance to the team.

The 24-year-old was signed from Ajax in 2018 and has now made over a century of appearances for the club.

Archie
GRAY
22

POSITION: Midfielder **COUNTRY:** England **DOB:** 12/03/2006

The great-nephew of Leeds United legend Eddie Gray, Archie Gray has now been handed the opportunity to shine in a first-team shirt by new manager Daniel Farke.

The skilful 17-year-old was given a starting place in the team on the opening day of the season and certainly did not look out of place. In Farke, the club have a manager with a tremendous track record of developing young talent and Gray looks all set to repay his manager's faith in him.

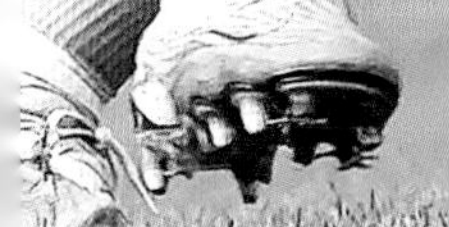

THE CHAMPIONSHIP SQUAD 2023/24

Georginio RUTTER 24

POSITION: Forward **COUNTRY:** France **DOB:** 20/04/2022

An exciting French under-21 international striker, Georginio Rutter became Leeds United's club record signing when he agreed a move to Elland Road from 1899 Hoffenheim in January 2023.

Rutter made his Whites debut in the club's FA Cup fourth round victory over Accrington Stanley. He featured in 11 Premier League fixtures last season and the club will be hopeful of seeing him among the goals in 2023/24 as Leeds aim for an instant return to the Premier League.

Sam BYRAM 25

POSITION: Defender **COUNTRY:** England **DOB:** 16/09/1993

Full-back Sam Byram saw his career go full circle when he agreed a one-year deal to rejoin Leeds United ahead of the 2023/24 season.

Byram began his career with Leeds as an Academy scholar in 2010 and went on to make almost 150 first-team appearances in his first spell at the club. He joined West Ham United in 2016 and later spent four years with Norwich City. It was while at Carrow Road that he first worked with current Leeds manager Daniel Farke.

Lewis **BATE** 26

POSITION: Midfielder **COUNTRY:** England **DOB:** 28/10/2002

Leeds United completed the signing of England Under-20 international Lewis Bate from Chelsea in the summer of 2021. He went on to make his debut against West Ham United in the FA Cup in January 2022, before making his Premier League debut a week later against the same opposition in a 3-2 victory at the London Stadium.

Last season, Bate continued his development away from Elland Road, spending the campaign with League One side Oxford United, where he made 35 appearances in all competitions.

Bate returned to West Yorkshire at the start of the 2023/24 season and made his first appearance under new manager Daniel Farke in the 2-1 EFL Cup victory over Shrewsbury Town at Elland Road.

Ian **POVEDA** 27

POSITION: Midfielder **COUNTRY:** England **DOB:** 09/02/2000

Attacking midfielder Ian Poveda joined Leeds United from Manchester City in January 2020 and celebrated both promotion to the Premier League and the Championship title in his first season at Elland Road.

With first-team opportunities in the Premier League hard to come by, the 23-year-old former England-20 international has since taken in loan spells with Blackburn Rovers and Blackpool. However, he now appears part of Daniel Farke's plans and looks set to focus on making a big impression on the first-team scene at Elland Road in 2023/24.

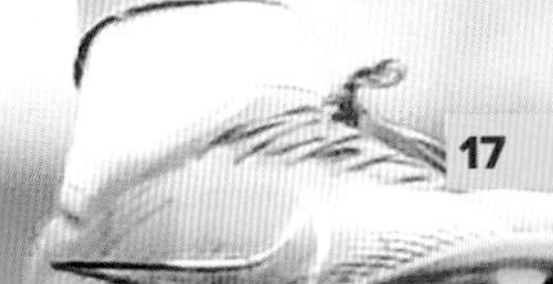

Karl **DARLOW** 28

POSITION: **Goalkeeper** COUNTRY: **England** DOB: **08/10/1990**

A much travelled and experienced goalkeeper, Karl Darlow joined Leeds United in the summer of 2023 from Newcastle United.

His arrival at Elland Road will certainly provide valued competition and cover in the goalkeeping department. Darlow's Leeds United debut came in the EFL Cup first-round victory over League One Shrewsbury Town as Daniel Farke's side defeated the Shrews 2-1 in front of over 35,000 fans at Elland Road.

Wilfried **GNONTO** 29

POSITION: **Forward** COUNTRY: **Italy** DOB: **05/11/2003**

Italian international forward Wilfried Gnonto is a real live-wire forward who joined Leeds United in the 2022 summer transfer window.

Signed from Swiss Super League champions FC Zurich, Gnonto netted four goals in his first season at Elland Road and his enthusiasm to make things happen in attacking areas has already made him very popular with supporters. The teenage sensation agreed a five-year deal when he joined the Whites and scored a memorable goal against arch rivals Manchester United at Old Trafford in the last campaign.

Joe **GELHARDT** 30

POSITION: Forward **COUNTRY:** England **DOB:** 04/05/2002

A powerfully built forward, Joe Gelhardt joined Leeds United in August 2020 from Wigan Athletic.

The youngster picked the perfect moment to score his first Elland Road goal, netting the most dramatic of last-gasp winners to secure three priceless Premier League points from a 2-1 victory over Norwich City in March 2022.

He gained valuable first-team experience with a loan to Sunderland last season and helped the Black Cats reach the end-of-season Play-Offs. He netted his first Leeds goal of 2023/24 in the EFL Cup victory over Shrewsbury Town.

Leo **HJELDE** 33

POSITION: Defender **COUNTRY:** Norway **DOB:** 26/08/2003

The Whites signed promising Norway under-21 international defender Leo Hjelde from Celtic in August 2021. The 6ft 2in defender made his Whites debut in January 2022 in an FA Cup third round match against West Ham United. His Premier League debut arrived a week later, also against the Hammers, when he became the youngest Norwegian to play in the Premier League.

Hjelde spent the second half of last season on loan with Rotherham United when he started 11 Championship matches to help keep the Millers in the second tier. The big Norwegian will now aim to make his mark with his parent club in 2023/24.

Djed **SPENCE**

39

POSITION: Defender **COUNTRY:** England **DOB:** 09/08/2000

England under-21 international defender Djed Spence joined the Leeds United ranks in August 2023 when he agreed a season-long loan deal at Elland Road.

The move sees the right-back reunite with his Tottenham Hotspur teammate Joe Rodon with both players switching North London for West Yorkshire in 2023/24. Spence knows what's needed to win promotion from the Championship having formed a vital part of Nottingham Forest's 2021/22 Play-Off winning side. It was his highly impressive performance for Forest, while on loan from Middlesbrough, that won him a big money move to Spurs in the summer of 2022.

THE CHAMPIONSHIP SQUAD 2023/24

Ilia GRUEV 44

POSITION: Midfielder **COUNTRY:** Bulgaria **DOB:** 06/05/2000

Leeds United bolstered their midfield options with the signing of Bulgarian international midfielder Ilia Gruev as the summer transfer window ended. The 23-year-old arrived at Elland Road from Werder Bremen and signed a four-year contract with Daniel Farke's side.

A defensive minded midfielder, Gruev's performances in the Bundesliga won rave reviews. His continued development in the game sees him following in his father's footsteps - Iliya Gruev - who was a Bulgarian international who won 13 caps for his country.

Mateo JOSEPH 49

POSITION: Forward **COUNTRY:** England **DOB:** 19/10/2003

An England under-20 international, Spain-born Mateo Joseph was a prolific scorer in the Espanyol youth system and his goals won him a move to Elland Road in January 2022.

Initially linking up with the under-21 squad at Thorp Arch, Joseph tasted EFL Cup, FA Cup and Premier League action for the first team last season. Turning 20 in October 2023, Joseph's strength and technical ability have already won him many admirers.

ONE OF THE HARDEST THINGS TO DO IN FOOTBALL IS TO STICK THE BALL IN THE BACK OF THE NET.

NOT LEAST BECAUSE THERE ARE USUALLY 11 OTHER PLAYERS TRYING TO STOP YOU DOING JUST THAT!

SHOOTING FROM DISTANCE

Good service is obviously important, and a good understanding with your striking partner is also vital, but when it comes to spectacular strikes, practice is the key to hitting a consistently accurate and powerful shot and to developing the timing and power required.

EXERCISE

A small-sided pitch is set up with two 18-yard boxes put together, but the corners of the pitch are cut off as shown in the diagram. There are five players per team, including goalkeepers, but only one player is allowed in the opponent's half.

The aim of the drill is to work a shooting opportunity when you have the ball, with the likely chance being to shoot from outside your opponent's penalty area, from distance. The teams take it in turns to release the ball into play from their own 'keeper - usually by rolling out to an unmarked player.

18 YDS

KEY FACTORS

1. **Attitude to shooting - be positive, have a go!**
2. **Technique - use laces, hit through the ball.**
3. **Do not sacrifice accuracy for power.**
4. **Wide angle shooting - aim for the far post.**
5. **Always follow up for rebounds!**

SOCCER SKILLS

The size of the pitch can be reduced for younger players, and it should be noted that these junior players should also be practicing with a size 4 or even a size 3 ball, depending on their age.

10

CRYSENCIO SUMMERVILLE

LEEDS UNITED WOMEN

LAURA BARTUP

In 2017, the women's team officially became part of the Leeds United umbrella once again and has continued to grow since.

Last season, under the management of Rick Passmoor, Leeds United Women created history by winning the FA Women's National League Plate, earning the club silverware for the first time in 13 years.

Goals from Macy Ellis, Abbie Brown and Amy Woodruff saw Leeds United Women defeat Stourbridge 3-1, bringing an end to a superb cup run that had seen Leeds beat teams from all over the country, including AFC Fylde and West Bromwich Albion from higher divisions.

For the 2023/24 season, Leeds United Women have moved grounds, from the So-Trak Stadium in Tadcaster, returning to their former home at Garforth's Bannister Prentice Stadium.

Also the home of Garforth Town AFC, the ground has newly refurbished facilities and is an added boost as Leeds United Women aim to embark on another exciting season, with an enhanced matchday experience for both players and fans.

Leeds United Women will compete in the Women's National League Division One North in the 2023/24 campaign and everyone wishes the club another successful season.

CHARLYANN PIZZARELLO

JESS ROUSSEAU CELEBRATES WITH TEAMMATES AFTER HER EQUALISER AGAINST STOCKPORT COUNTY LADIES.

DANIELLE WHITHAM HITS THE WINNER!

DAZZLING DEFENDERS

JACK CHARLTON, NORMAN HUNTER AND LUCAS RADEBE WERE ALL OUTSTANDING LEEDS DEFENDERS. CONTINUING THE TRADITION IS CURRENT UNITED STAR LUKE AYLING.

Jack Charlton was a legend in every sense of the word. A working class hero, a one-club man and a World Cup winner with England, he represents a piece of club history that Leeds United are exceptionally proud of.

He spent an incredible 21 years of his life playing for the Whites, proving a key figure in winning multiple domestic and European titles, but also remaining loyal to the club when falling upon hard times.

Described as 'granite-hard and belligerent', both in playing style and mentality, he was a rock at the back during Leeds' most successful-ever era.

JACK CHARLTON

DATE OF BIRTH: May 8, 1935

PLACE OF BIRTH: Ashington

NATIONALITY: English

LEEDS UNITED APPEARANCES: 773

LEEDS UNITED GOALS: 96

LEEDS UNITED DEBUT: April 25, 1953
Leeds United 1-1 Doncaster Rovers (Second Division)

With a nickname of "Bites Yer Legs," forwards knew what they were in for when they faced up to Norman Hunter. That wasn't to be taken literally, of course - it was a reference to his snappy, firm tackles that set a firm tone in games!

Hunter spent more than a decade at the heart of Leeds United's defence, standing loyally next to Jack Charlton and repelling attacks from every angle.

The success that Leeds enjoyed during this period was no coincidence, while Hunter was also regularly called up for England and collected a 1966 World Cup winner's medal.

NORMAN HUNTER

DATE OF BIRTH: October 29, 1943

PLACE OF BIRTH: Gateshead

NATIONALITY: English

LEEDS UNITED APPEARANCES: 726

LEEDS UNITED GOALS: 21

LEEDS UNITED DEBUT: September 8, 1962
Swansea Town 0-2 Leeds United (Second Division)

Described by the late, great, Nelson Mandela as his very own "hero", Lucas Radebe is a legend at Leeds United. Known affectionately as "The Chief," following his move to Elland Road from the Kaizer Chiefs in 1994, Radebe went on to become one of the best defenders to have ever played for the club.

Made captain of Leeds United in 1998, Radebe also captained South Africa at the 1998 FIFA World Cup and the 2002 FIFA World Cup and he won a total of 70 caps for his country. In 2000 he was also awarded the FIFA Fair Play Award for his efforts in reducing racism in football.

One of the best central defenders in his era, Radebe further enhanced his reputation with Leeds supporters, by turning down transfers to a number of clubs, to remain loyal to the Whites. He retired in 2005, having made 262 appearances for the Whites.

LUCAS RADEBE

DATE OF BIRTH: April 12, 1969

PLACE OF BIRTH: Soweto, South Africa

NATIONALITY: South African

LEEDS UNITED APPEARANCES: 262

LEEDS UNITED GOALS: 3

LEEDS UNITED DEBUT: September 26, 1994
Sheffield Wednesday 1-1 Leeds United (Premier League)

LUKE AYLING

DATE OF BIRTH: August 25, 1991

PLACE OF BIRTH: London

NATIONALITY: English

LEEDS UNITED APPEARANCES: 252*

LEEDS UNITED GOALS: 10*

LEEDS UNITED DEBUT: August 13, 2016
Leeds United 1-2 Birmingham City (EFL Championship)

*AS AT THE END OF THE 2022/23 SEASON

Secured for just £200,000, Luke Ayling represents one of the modern bargains of the game. Over 200 appearances later, he's proved that fee to be a pittance.

He's been a constant factor in the defensive line since 2016, flying up and down the flank from right-back, but also stepping in at centre-back too. He's scored some great goals, some important goals, and emerged as a key player.

That quality, in addition to his larger-than-life personality, has endeared him to the Elland Road crowd.

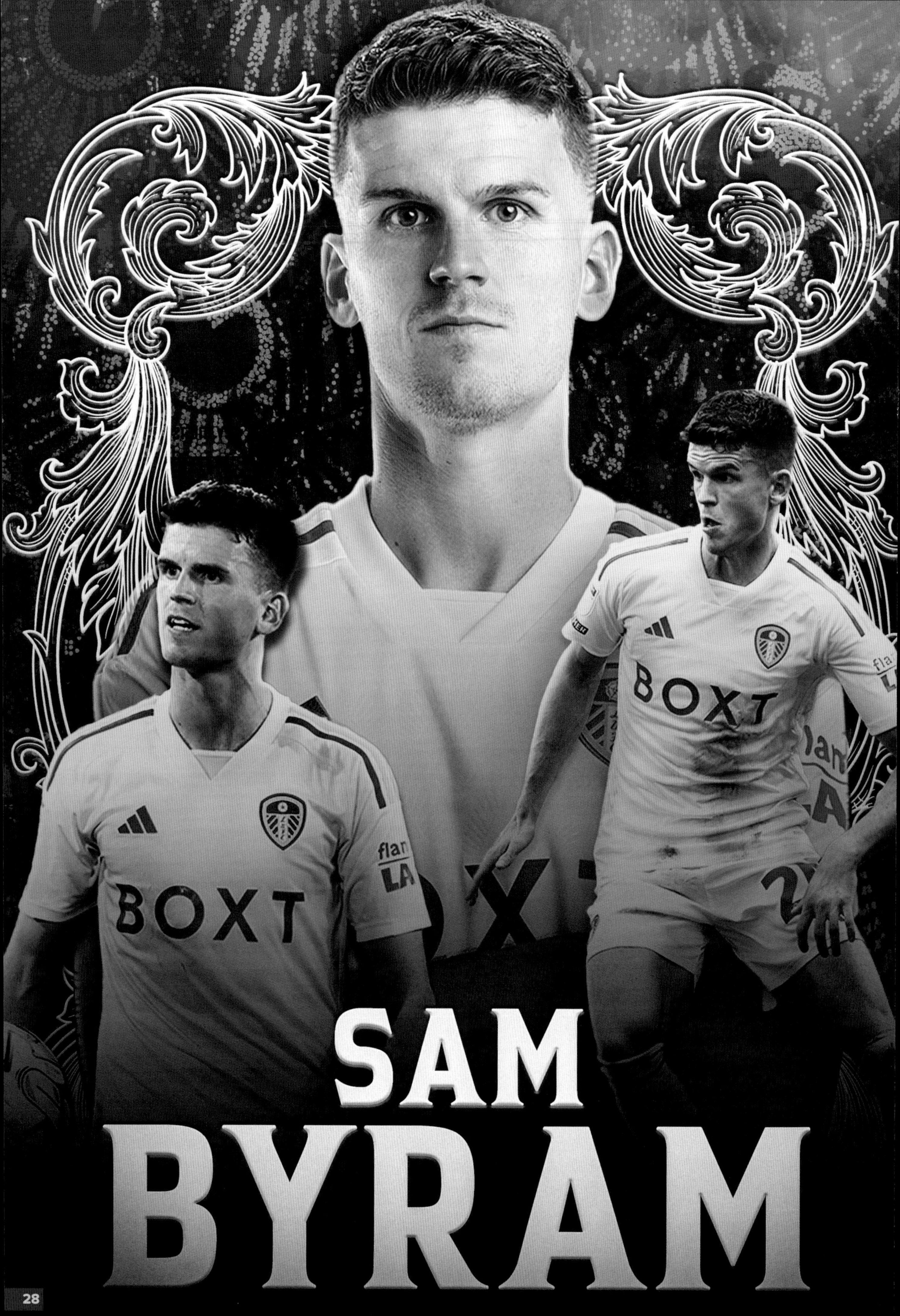
BOXT
BOXT
SAM
BYRAM

FOOTY PHRASES

ALL OF THESE FOOTY PHRASES ARE HIDDEN IN THE GRID, EXCEPT FOR ONE ...BUT CAN YOU WORK OUT WHICH ONE?

ANSWERS ON PAGE 62

C	A	E	S	W	Y	V	Y	B	H	U	G	N	U	R	Y	M	M	U	D
V	U	Q	I	D	E	R	B	Y	D	A	Y	O	L	U	R	T	S	S	U
K	F	A	D	J	L	G	T	X	T	F	C	B	E	I	A	K	C	F	P
I	B	H	E	O	T	L	P	Z	R	V	N	M	W	O	J	I	R	Y	A
C	M	O	F	F	S	I	D	E	R	U	L	E	E	D	S	P	E	Y	H
M	E	R	U	E	I	J	R	D	E	D	A	Q	G	S	H	L	A	X	C
R	X	E	R	N	H	A	T	T	R	I	C	K	O	I	L	A	M	R	T
E	I	Y	O	W	W	S	L	S	N	O	W	R	S	O	Z	Y	E	Y	A
D	C	A	A	Z	L	W	S	J	K	T	K	Y	V	K	B	M	R	T	M
A	A	L	P	X	A	U	Y	H	M	I	D	F	I	E	D	A	R	O	E
E	N	P	T	K	N	F	W	G	C	P	L	J	K	A	M	K	N	L	H
H	W	E	J	A	I	L	O	K	H	A	O	F	O	H	I	E	C	G	T
G	A	M	E	O	F	T	W	O	H	A	L	V	E	S	T	R	N	U	F
N	V	A	I	A	H	E	S	L	F	J	D	U	A	O	I	U	O	T	O
I	E	G	B	I	C	L	A	S	S	A	C	T	U	P	F	G	E	V	N
V	D	G	O	A	E	E	U	C	K	S	S	C	Y	W	U	L	Q	L	A
I	R	I	R	Q	G	M	N	S	A	C	H	G	H	D	O	S	F	G	M
D	V	B	A	C	K	O	F	T	H	E	N	E	T	Z	P	X	B	N	A

Back of the Net
Big Game Player
Brace
Class Act
Derby Day
Diving Header
Dugout
Dummy Run
Final Whistle
Game of Two Halves
Half Volley
Hat-trick
Keepie Uppie
Man of the Match
Mexican Wave
Offside Rule
One-touch
Playmaker
Scissor Kick
Screamer

THE GENERATION GAME

ANDY

POSITION: Forward
DOB: 15 November 1977
FAMILY TIE: Son of Frank, nephew of Eddie, father of Archie.
DID YOU KNOW? Gray had two spells as a player at Elland Road from 1995-1998 and 2012-2013.

For many generations of the Elland Road faithful, following the fortunes of Leeds United is often very much a family affair. While everyone has their own tale of why they support the Whites, the chances are that it was perhaps the influence of a parent, grandparent, auntie, or uncle that played a part in introducing you to life at Elland Road.

Young supporters attending their first match with family members and becoming the next generation of Leeds United supporters is a common and heartwarming sight on matchday.

Following in family footsteps and backing the team home and away has become a ritual for many families of passionate Leeds fans.

For one particular teenager, his family's association with Leeds United goes a little further than just supporting the Whites. The young man in questions is Leeds United's 17-year-old midfield starlet Archie Gray.

Handed squad No.22 for the 2023/24 campaign, Archie continued a phenomenal family connection with Leeds United when he made his first-team debut in the Whites' opening game of the 2023/24 season.

Archie follows in the footsteps of his father Andy who also began his playing career with the Whites and ended up having two spells as a first-team player at Elland Road.

However, the family's connections run far deeper than just a father and son playing for the same club. Archie's grandad is Frank Gray who himself starred for the club in the 1970s. And the family circle is completed with Archie also being the great nephew of Leeds United legend Eddie Gray.

So, when Archie pulls on a Leeds United shirt, suffice to say there is a fair weight of expectation and reputation on his young shoulders.

As anyone who was witnessed Archie's development via the Academy teams will know, he is clearly a player blessed with a great deal of natural ability, confidence and flair. The icing on the cake for him right now is that he is playing for a manager with a great reputation of developing young players and putting trust in young talent. As head coach of Norwich City, Daniel Farke honed the skills of Max Aarons, Ben Godfrey, Jamal Lewis and Todd Cantwell while twice leading Norwich City to the Championship title.

The stage is certainly set for Archie to go on and further enhance his family's Leeds United dynasty and it's fair to say the odd useful word of advice will never be too far away.

EDDIE & FRANK

POSITION: Winger
DOB: 17 January 1948
FAMILY TIE: Elder brother of Frank, uncle to Andy, great uncle to Archie.
DID YOU KNOW? In a loyal one-club playing career Eddie made a colossal 577 appearances for Leeds United.

POSITION: Full-back
DOB: 27 October 1954
FAMILY TIE: Younger brother of Eddie, father of Andy and grandfather of Archie.
DID YOU KNOW? A member of the 1973/74 First Division title-winning team, Frank had two separate spells as a player at Elland Road.

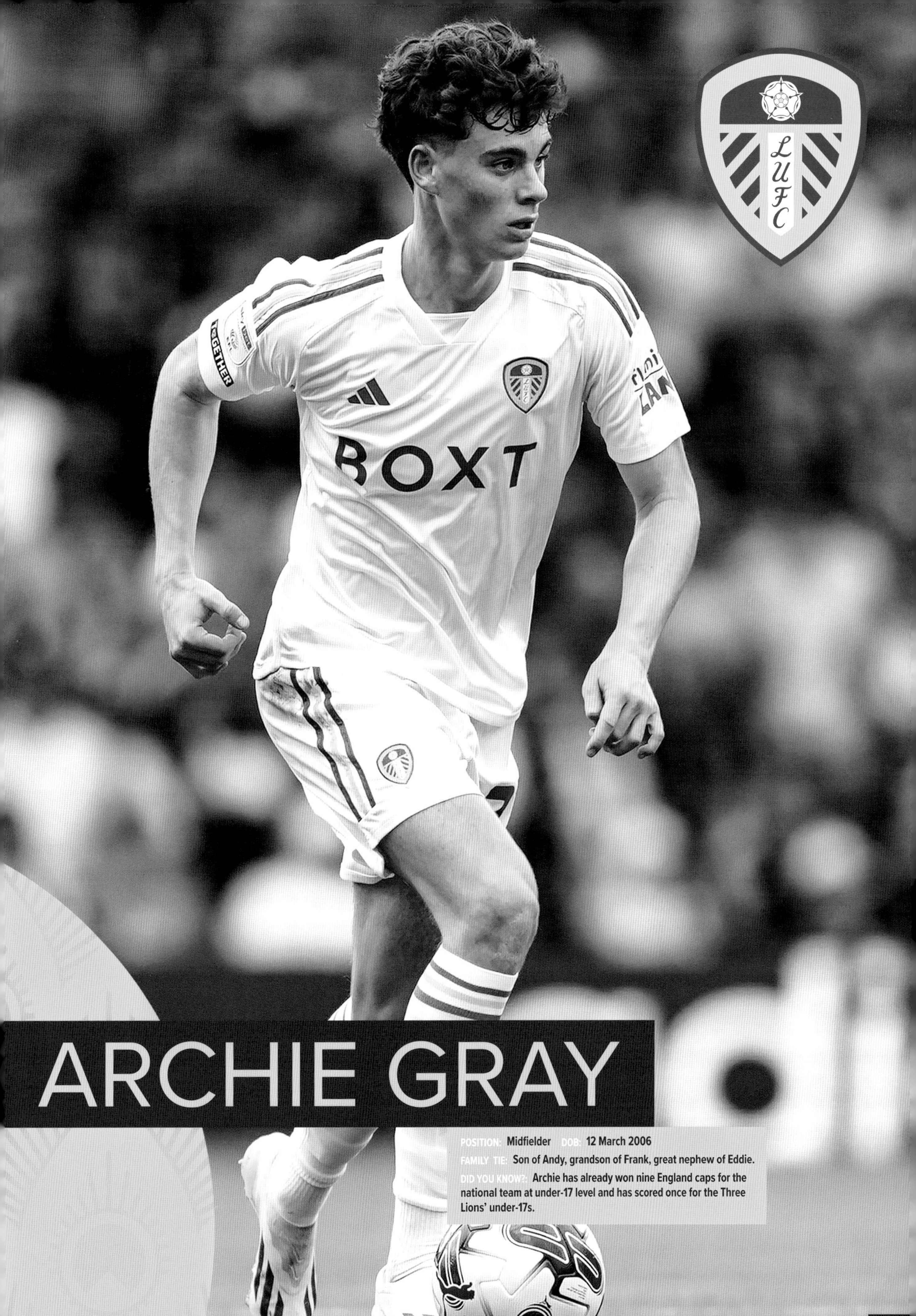

ARCHIE GRAY

POSITION: Midfielder **DOB:** 12 March 2006

FAMILY TIE: Son of Andy, grandson of Frank, great nephew of Eddie.

DID YOU KNOW?: Archie has already won nine England caps for the national team at under-17 level and has scored once for the Three Lions' under-17s.

TOP CLASS PLAYERS NOT ONLY NEED TO WIN THE BALL IN MIDFIELD, BUT ALSO PROVIDE THAT CUTTING EDGE WHEN NEEDED TO BE ABLE TO PLAY THROUGH DEFENCES WITH QUICK, INCISIVE PASSING.

THE WALL PASS

With teams being very organised in modern football, it can be very difficult to break them down and create scoring opportunities. One of the best ways to achieve this is by using the 'wall pass', otherwise known as the quick one-two.

EXERCISE

In a non-pressurised situation, involving four players, A carries the ball forward towards a static defender (in this case a cone) and before reaching the defender, plays the ball to B before running around the opposite side to receive the one-touch return pass. A then delivers the ball safely to C who then repeats the exercise returning the ball to D, and in this way the exercise continues. Eventually a defender can be used to make the exercise more challenging, with all players being rotated every few minutes.

The exercise can progress into a five-a-side game, the diagram below shows how additional players (W) on the touchline can be used as 'walls' with just one touch available to help the man in possession of the ball.

Each touchline player can move up and down the touchline, but not enter the pitch - they can also play for either team.

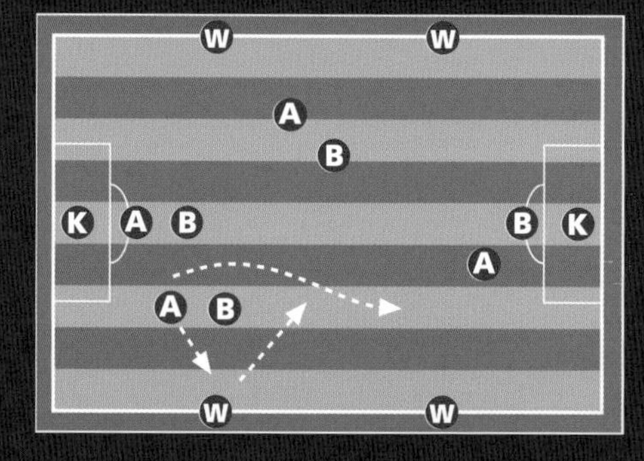

KEY FACTORS

1. **Look to commit the defender before passing - do not play the ball too early.**
2. **Pass the ball firmly and to feet.**
3. **Accelerate past defender after passing.**
4. **Receiver (B) make themselves available for the pass.**
5. **B delivers a return pass, weighted correctly, into space.**

SOCCER SKILLS

If done correctly, this is a tactic which is extremely difficult to stop, but needs teamwork and communication between the two attacking players.

STAND
BOXT
R F W
22

A-Z

ARE YOU READY TO TACKLE OUR A-Z FOOTBALL QUIZ?

THE SIMPLE RULE IS THAT THE ANSWERS RUN THROUGH THE 26 LETTERS OF THE ALPHABET.

A

What nationality is Watford goalkeeper Daniel Bachmann?

A

B

Which team won the Sky Bet Championship title in 2022/23?

B

C

Which Premier League club reappointed their former manager as interim boss in March 2023?

C

D

Which League One side play their home matches at Pride Park?

D

E

What nationality is Liverpool's sensational striker Mohamed Salah?

E

F

Which country knocked England out of the FIFA World Cup finals in 2022?

F

Which famous football ground is due to host its final fixture in 2024?

G

H Which club did Neil Warnock lead to Championship survival in 2022/23?

H

I Which country did England defeat 6-2 in their opening game of the FIFA 2022 World Cup finals?

I

J Aston Villa winger Leon Bailey plays internationally for which country?

J

K What is the name of Premier League new boys Luton Town's home ground?

K

L Can you name the Ipswich Town striker who netted 17 League One goals in the Tractor Boys' 2022/23 promotion-winning season?

L

M **Which Championship club boasted the division's top scorer in 2022/23?**

M

ANSWERS ON PAGE 62

N

What nationality is Manchester City's ace marksman Erling Haaland?

N

O

Can you name the former Premier League team that will compete in the National League in 2023/24?

O

P

Which international striker ended five seasons with Norwich City in May 2023?

P

Q

Can you name the country that hosted the FIFA 2022 World Cup finals?

Q

R

Which Spanish side did Manchester City defeat in last season's UEFA Champions League semi-final?

R

S

Which team knocked Premier League champions Manchester City out of the Carabao Cup last season?

S

T

Which full-back left Huddersfield Town to join Nottingham Forest ahead of their return to the Premier League in the summer of 2022?

T

A-Z PART TWO

U **Can you name Brighton's German forward who joined the Seagulls in January 2022?**

U

V Can you name the former England striker who has hit over 100 Premier League goals for Leicester City?

V

W Can you name the goalkeeper who got his name on the scoresheet last season in a Championship fixture?

W

X Can you name the Portuguese international defender who played in the Premier League with Everton, Liverpool & Middlesbrough?

X

Y At which club did Leeds United's Luke Ayling make his league debut?

Y

Z **Which Dutch international midfielder played Premier League football for Chelsea, Middlesbrough and Liverpool in the 2000s?**

Z

ANSWERS ON PAGE 62

JOËL PIROE

DESIGN A FOOTY BOOT

Design a brilliant new footy boot for the Leeds United squad!

MIDFIELD MAESTROS

BILLY BREMNER, GARY SPEED AND PABLO HERNANDEZ WERE ALL GREAT LEEDS MAESTROS AND LOOKING TO CONTINUE THAT PROUD TREND IS ETHAN AMPADU.

Billy Bremner fought the battle all too many footballers have over the years, as he was deemed too short (5'5") by many top clubs until Leeds United picked him up.

He grew into a crucial presence in midfield during Leeds' most successful ever period, with manager Don Revie remarking "no manager could wish for a greater leader or a greater player."

Lauded for his blend of pinpoint passing and competitive, fiery energy, he gained international recognition for his incredible feats at Elland Road. Closer to home, he's held in even higher regard, voted the greatest player in Leeds history.

BILLY BREMNER

DATE OF BIRTH: December 9, 1942

PLACE OF BIRTH: Stirling, Scotland

NATIONALITY: Scottish

LEEDS UNITED APPEARANCES: 772

LEEDS UNITED GOALS: 115

LEEDS UNITED DEBUT: January 23, 1960
Chelsea 1-3 Leeds United (First Division)

Gary Speed was part of a great Leeds United team in 1992, they won the title thanks in part to a remarkable midfield quartet, of which Speed was the key protagonist.

After initially playing a variety of positions while breaking into the team, he truly blossomed on the left flank, charging up and down with equal parts guile and gusto. He saw the game beautifully and boasted incredible stamina and conditioning, allowing him to play virtually every game in the calendar.

His ability and character is held in the highest esteem across the sport in the United Kingdom and beyond.

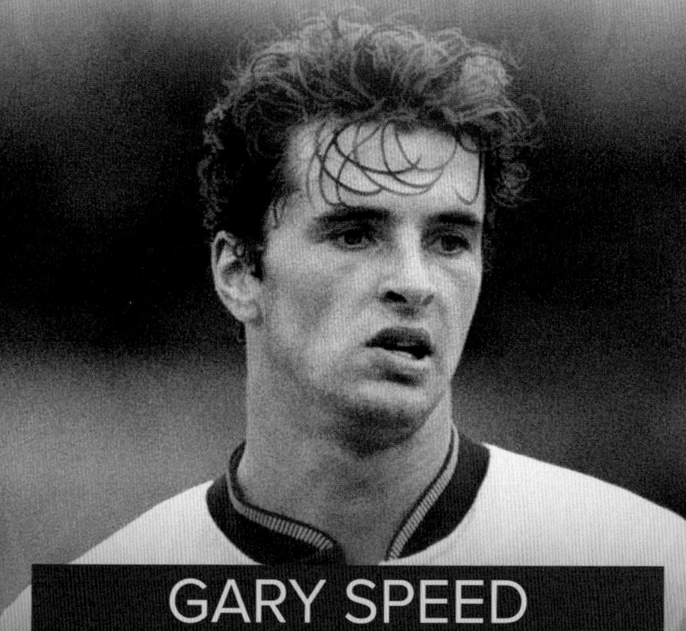

GARY SPEED

DATE OF BIRTH: September 8, 1969

PLACE OF BIRTH: Mancot, Wales

NATIONALITY: Welsh

LEEDS UNITED APPEARANCES: 312

LEEDS UNITED GOALS: 57

LEEDS UNITED DEBUT: August 15, 1989
Oldham Athletic 2-1 Leeds United (Second Division)

"A complete player from every point of view" was Marcelo Bielsa's assessment of Pablo Hernandez, who became a crucial player under his tenure and perhaps the pivotal performer in the 2019/20 promotion season.

That suggestion is cemented by the fact he scored the goal that effectively sealed promotion - a clever, 89th-minute finish at Swansea City - capping a glorious run of form to finish the campaign.

He was the heartbeat of a team who played dominant football, scored great goals and achieved great things. Leeds fans just wish he had found his way to them a few years earlier!

PABLO HERNANDEZ

DATE OF BIRTH: April 11, 1985

PLACE OF BIRTH: Castellón, Spain

NATIONALITY: Spanish

LEEDS UNITED APPEARANCES: 175

LEEDS UNITED GOALS: 36

LEEDS UNITED DEBUT: March 21, 2006
Leeds United 0-1 Crystal Palace (EFL Championship)

ETHAN AMPADU

DATE OF BIRTH: September 14, 2000

PLACE OF BIRTH: Exeter

NATIONALITY: Welsh

LEEDS UNITED APPEARANCES: 7*

LEEDS UNITED GOALS: 0*

LEEDS UNITED DEBUT: August 6, 2023
Leeds United 2-2 Cardiff City (Championship)

*AS AT SEPTEMBER 2, 2023

Recruited from Chelsea, Ethan Ampadu became the club's first signing of the summer transfer window ahead of the 2023/24 season and the first of the Daniel Farke era.

Starting the new season as a key man in the holding role, Ampadu has already endeared himself to the Leeds United supporters with some very impressive displays. With his tenacious tackling and ability to spread the ball effortlessly, his signing appears to be some astute business.

With experience of the Premier League and Serie A in Italy, along with over 40 international caps to his name with Wales at the age of just 23, the 2023/24 campaign could be one to remember for the midfielder.

KOP CAT

Lucas the Kop Cat is hiding in the Elland Road crowd in five different places with Leeds United fans in full voice earlier this season.

Can you find all five?

FAN'TASTIC

ANSWERS ON PAGE 62

LUFC

ILLAN MESLIER

WHICH...

Can you figure out which football is the real one in each of these photos?

A
B
C
D
E
F
G
H

...BALL?

ANSWERS ON PAGE 62

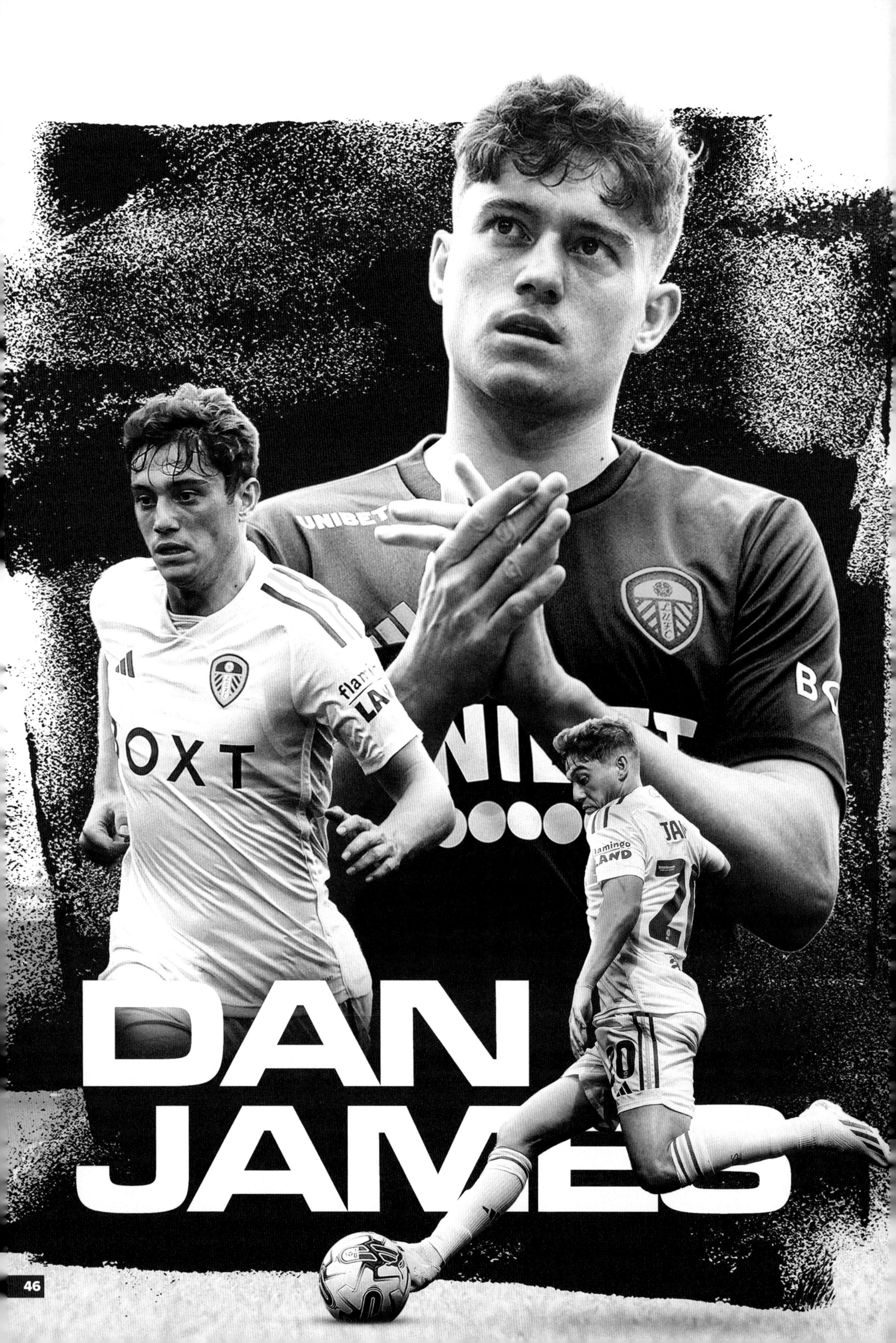
DAN
JAMES

SPOT...

Can you find the eight differences between these two celebration photos?

ANSWERS ON PAGE 62

...THE DIFFERENCE

BEHIND THE BADGE

CAN YOU IDENTIFY EVERY ONE OF THESE LEEDS STARS...

...HIDDEN BEHIND OUR BEAUTIFUL BADGE?

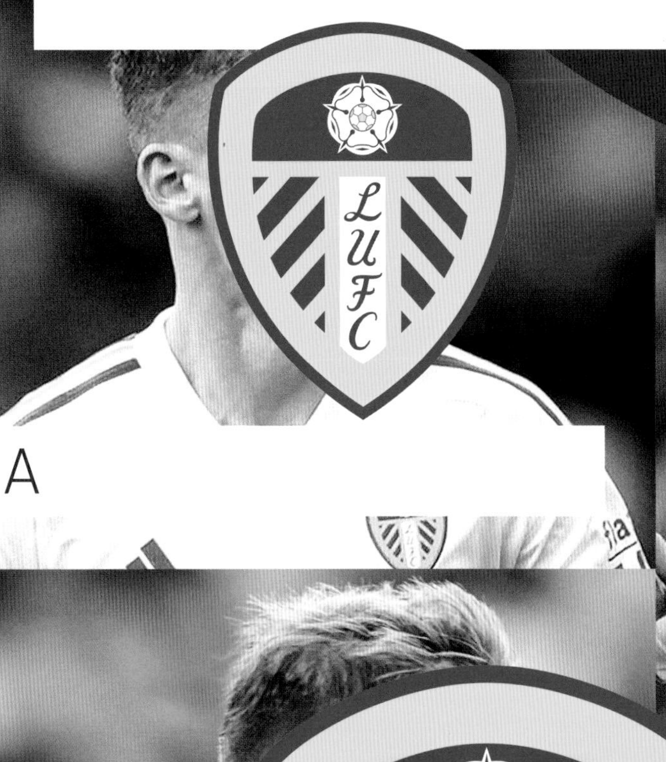

A

B

C

ANSWERS ON PAGE 62

BOXT
BOXT
AMPADU
4
ETHAN
AMPADU

TRUE COLOURS

HAVE FUN COLOURING IN THIS PICTURE OF LEEDS STAR
ETHAN AMPADU

STUNNING STRIKERS

ALLAN CLARKE, LEE CHAPMAN AND TONY YEBOAH WERE ALL ACE MARKSMEN FOR LEEDS UNITED AND FOLLOWING IN THEIR FOOTSTEPS IS SUPER STRIKER PATRICK BAMFORD.

Hailed as the final, missing piece, Allan Clarke 'completed' Don Revie's legendary Leeds United side upon joining in 1969.

Affectionately nicknamed 'Sniffer' thanks to his prowess in the penalty box, constantly latching onto half-chances and stray balls and turning them into goals, his style was typical of the era - but he pulled it off better than almost anyone else.

Clarke hit double figures for goals in seven straight seasons - twice scoring a whopping 26 times - en route to a bundle of silverware in Leeds white, cementing his status as a striking great for the club.

ALLAN CLARKE

DATE OF BIRTH: July 31, 1946

PLACE OF BIRTH: Staffordshire

NATIONALITY: English

LEEDS UNITED APPEARANCES: 366

LEEDS UNITED GOALS: 151

LEEDS UNITED DEBUT: August 2, 1969
Leeds United 2-1 Manchester City (FA Charity Shield)

Sometimes, all a footballer needs is to find the right manager, and in Howard Wilkinson, Lee Chapman found exactly that.

Wilkinson signed him for Leeds United in 1990 having already managed him at Sheffield Wednesday, so therefore understood how to unleash his ruthless, prolific style inside the penalty box from the get-go.

He hit the ground running in January, then scored 31 in his first full season with the Whites. After that came the crowning achievement: scoring 20 in 1991/92 as they won the First Division title, spearheading a fearsome team and offering a vital outlet up top.

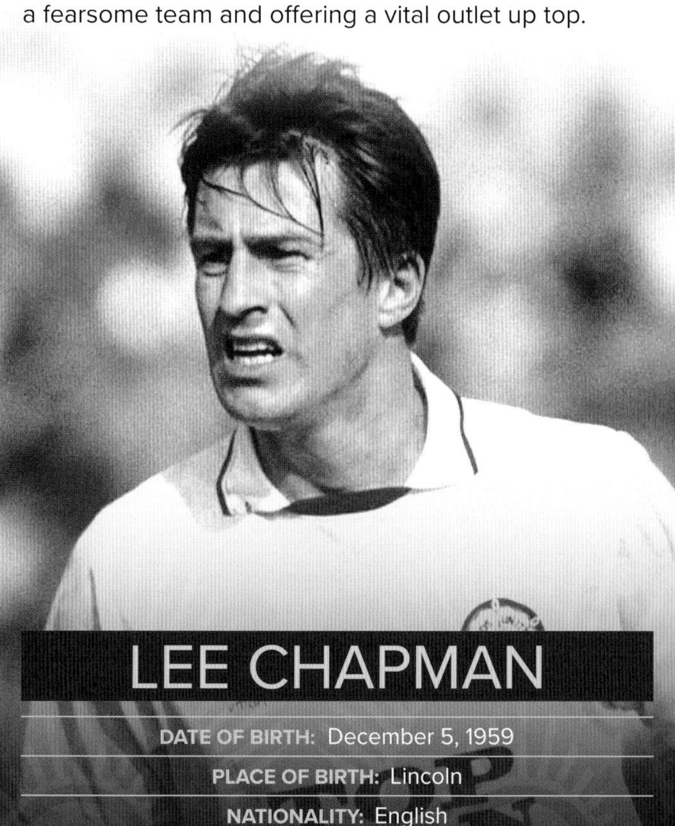

LEE CHAPMAN

DATE OF BIRTH: December 5, 1959

PLACE OF BIRTH: Lincoln

NATIONALITY: English

LEEDS UNITED APPEARANCES: 175

LEEDS UNITED GOALS: 80

LEEDS UNITED DEBUT: January 13, 1990
Blackburn Rovers 1-2 Leeds United (Second Division)

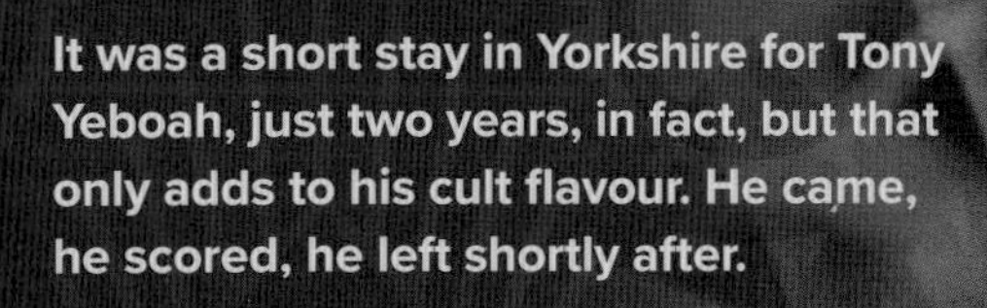

It was a short stay in Yorkshire for Tony Yeboah, just two years, in fact, but that only adds to his cult flavour. He came, he scored, he left shortly after.

It was back at a time where arrivals from abroad carried a true level of mystique and unknown. Whatever fans were expecting from the Ghanaian, it almost certainly wasn't what he delivered.

Barely a month went by without a Goal of the Month competition featuring one of his wonderful feats, be it mazy dribble and finishes or long-range screamers. Fans remember his thumping volley against Liverpool and his iconic hat-trick against Monaco, among many others!

TONY YEBOAH

DATE OF BIRTH: June 6, 1966

PLACE OF BIRTH: Kumasi, Ghana

NATIONALITY: Ghanaian

LEEDS UNITED APPEARANCES: 66

LEEDS UNITED GOALS: 32

LEEDS UNITED DEBUT: January 21, 1995
Leeds United 4-0 Derby County (Premier League)

PATRICK BAMFORD

DATE OF BIRTH: September 5, 1993

PLACE OF BIRTH: Grantham

NATIONALITY: English

LEEDS UNITED APPEARANCES: 151*

LEEDS UNITED GOALS: 51*

LEEDS UNITED DEBUT: August 11, 2018
Derby County 1-4 Leeds United (EFL Championship)

AS AT THE END OF THE 2022/23 SEASON

Patrick Bamford has blossomed into a striker who has commanded the Leeds United attack during their best spell just shy of two decades.

He plundered 16 goals in 2019/20 and led the team to promotion from the front, then scored an incredible 17 in the Whites' first season back in the Premier League for 17 years.

His ability to lead the line, defend from the front and find the corners when shooting were crucial to the team over this period. Leeds is where Patrick Bamford finally found a home.

>>FAST

Norwich City (HOME)

SKY BET CHAMPIONSHIP • JANUARY 27, 2024

The opening month of 2024 will see Leeds' boss Daniel Farke go head-to-head with his former club when Norwich City provide the Elland Road opposition on January 27.

Now in their second season outside of the Premier League, a level that Fake twice guided the Canaries to, Norwich suffered a highly disappointing 2022/23 campaign at Championship level and will be looking for a vast improvement in fortunes in 2024.

The Canaries have added a lot of experience to their ranks including former Burnley striker Ashley Barnes and their visit to Elland Road is sure to be an interesting affair as Farke takes on fellow German coach David Wagner.

Leicester City (HOME)

SKY BET CHAMPIONSHIP • FEBRUARY 24, 2024

One of the standout fixtures at Elland Road in 2024 must be the February visit of Leicester City. Relegated alongside the Whites last season, the Foxes' squad remains packed with quality performers and is now under the management of former Manchester City coach Enzo Maresca.

Despite dropping into the Championship, recent times have seen Leicester City enjoy the most successful period in the club's history - the Foxes were crowned Premier League champions in 2016 and FA Cup winners in 2021.

Leicester City will be among the favourites for an instant return to the Premier League and began the season in great form by winning their opening two games of the season.

Huddersfield Town (AWAY)

SKY BET CHAMPIONSHIP • MARCH 2, 2024

Leeds United's busy month of March starts with the short trip to face West Yorkshire rivals Huddersfield Town at the John Smith's Stadium on March 2.

While Huddersfield had a tough start to the season, they showed their worth with an excellent win away to WBA in September, then returned to action after the international break with a vital 2-0 home victory over Rotherham United to really kick-start their campaign. With Dutch forward Delano Burgzorg on a season-long loan from Mainz and midfielder Ben Wiles looking an inspired summer signing from Rotherham, the Terriers are sure to provide tough opposition for Leeds United with both Championship points and Yorkshire pride at stake.

FORWARD

SIX BIG CHAMPIONSHIP ENCOUNTERS TO LOOK FORWARD TO IN 2024...

Coventry City (AWAY)

SKY BET CHAMPIONSHIP • APRIL 6, 2024

Coventry City found themselves penalty kicks away from promotion to the Premier League last season and after suffering the cruellest of endings to the 2022/23 season, the Sky Blues will be keen to go all the way in 2023/24.

Under the management of Mark Robins, Coventry are a proven force at Championship level and our match at the Coventry Arena in April is certain to be a true test of the Whites' promotion credentials.

Despite the sale of star men Viktor Gyokeres and Gus Hamer, Coventry have made several exciting additions to their squad for the current campaign including American forward Haji Wright and former Everton striker Ellis Simms.

Sunderland (HOME)

SKY BET CHAMPIONSHIP • APRIL 9, 2024

Tony Mowbray will bring his exciting young Sunderland team to Elland Road for a midweek fixture on April 9 as the 2023/24 season potentially reaches boiling point.

The visitors enjoyed an impressive Championship campaign last time out securing sixth spot in the table, only to be beaten by eventual Play-Off winners Luton Town at the semi-final stage.

Looking build on their success from last season, the Black Cats showed their Championship capabilities with an impressive early season 5-0 rout of Southampton at the Stadium of Light - a match which saw former Leeds United man Jack Clarke open the scoring.

Southampton (HOME)

SKY BET CHAMPIONSHIP • MAY 4, 2024

Southampton completed the trio of teams relegated from the Premier League in 2022/23 and are sure to provide a tough challenge at Elland Road on the final day of 2023/24.

The Saints are another club that made a managerial change in the summer of 2023 with former MK Dons and Swansea City head coach Russell Martin being the man appointed to spearhead their promotion ambitions for 2023/24.

Early season form indicated that the Saints could well be the division's great entertainers after an opening night 2-1 victory at Sheffield Wednesday was followed by an astonishing 4-4 draw at home to Norwich City.

BEING PREDICTABLE IS EASY IN FOOTBALL.

DOING THE UNEXPECTED IS A LOT MORE DIFFICULT.

TURNING WITH THE BALL

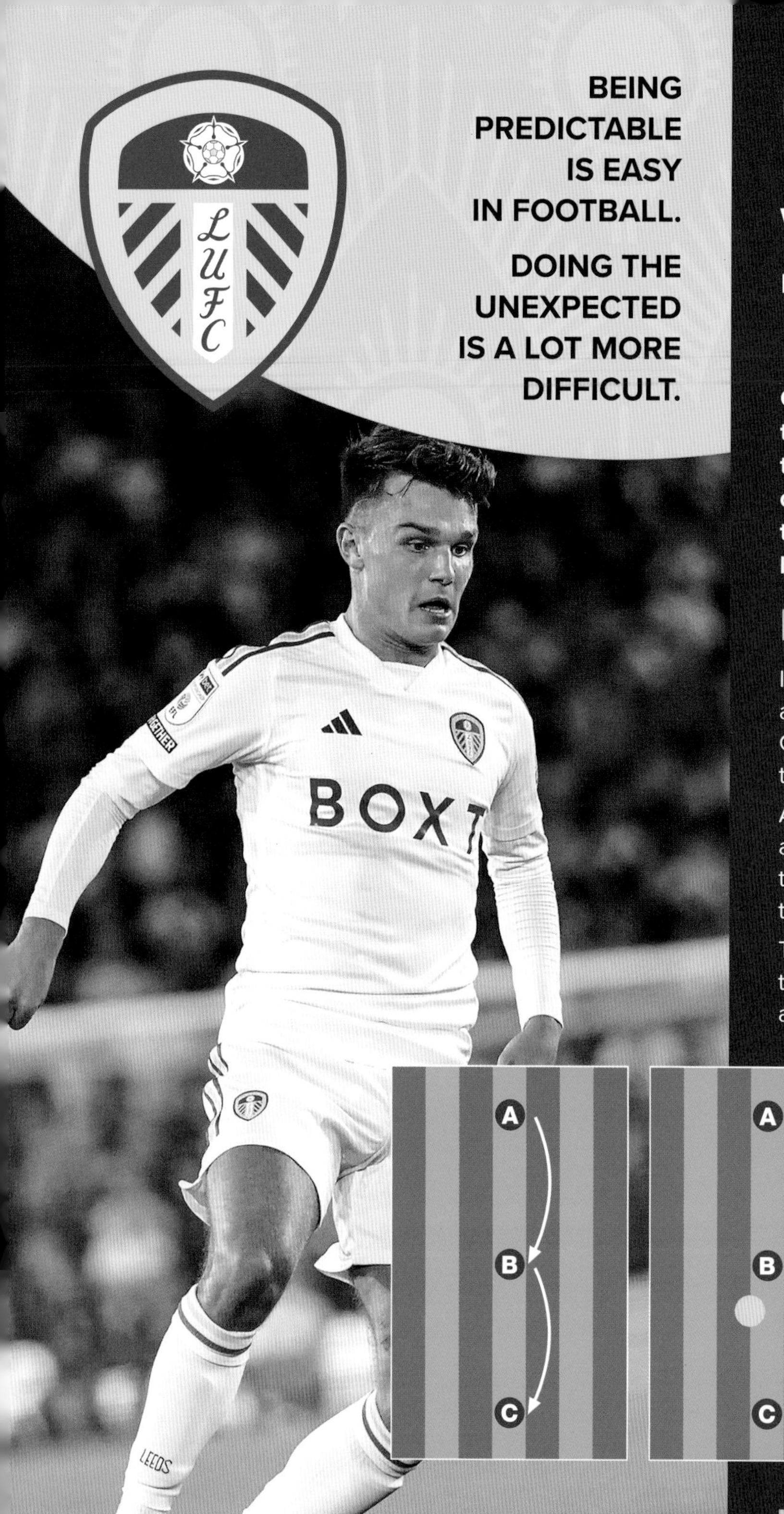

One of the biggest problems a defence can have to deal with is when a skilful player is prepared to turn with the ball and run at them, committing a key defender into making a challenge. Because football today is so fast and space so precious, this is becoming a rare skill.

EXERCISE 1

In an area 20m x 10m, A plays the ball into B who turns, and with two touches maximum plays the ball into C. C controls and reverses the process. After a few minutes the middleman is changed.

As you progress, a defender is brought in to oppose B, and is initially encouraged to play a 'passive' role. B has to turn and play the ball to C who is allowed to move along the baseline.

The type of turns can vary. Players should be encouraged to use the outside of the foot, inside of the foot, with feint and disguise to make space for the turn.

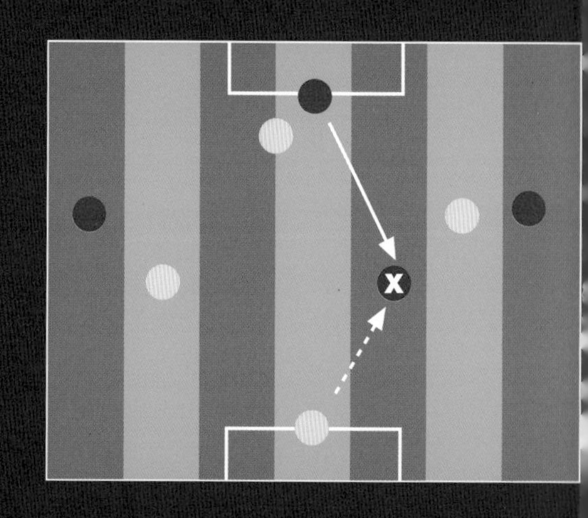

EXERCISE 2

As the players grow in confidence, you can move forward to a small-sided game. In this example of a 4-a-side practice match, X has made space for himself to turn with the ball, by coming off his defender at an angle. By doing this he can see that the defender has not tracked him, and therefore has the awareness to turn and attack.

SOCCER SKILLS

Matches at the top level are won and lost by pieces of skill such as this, so players have to be brave enough to go in search of the ball, and turn in tight situations.

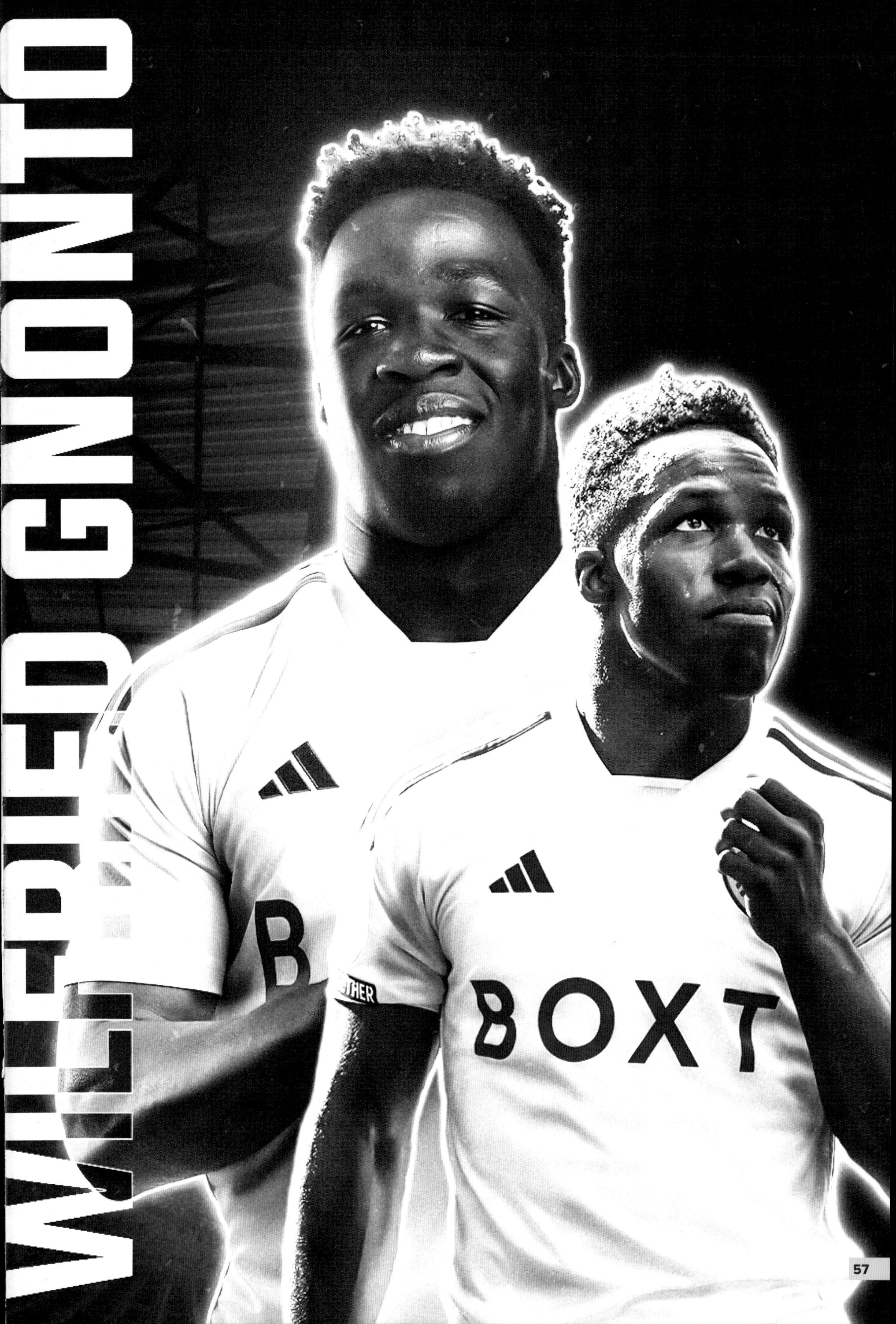

WILFRED GNONTO

HIGH FIVES

TEST YOUR LEEDS UNITED KNOWLEDGE & MEMORY WITH OUR HIGH FIVES QUIZ

1. Across the previous five seasons, who have been Leeds United's leading league goalscorers?

1.
2.
3.
4.
5.

2. Can you name the Whites' last five FA Cup opponents ahead of the 2023/24 season?

1.
2.
3.
4.
5.

3. Prior to Daniel Farke, who were Leeds United's last five permanent managers?

1.
2.
3.
4.
5.

4. Can you name our last five EFL Cup opponents as at the end of the 2022/23 season?

1.
2.
3.
4.
5.

5. Can you name the trophies that Leeds United won in the following seasons?

1. 2019/20
2. 1991/92
3. 1989/90
4. 1973/74
5. 1971/72

8. Can you recall the scoreline and season from our last five victories over rivals Manchester United?

1.
2.
3.
4.
5.

6. Which Leeds players started the most league fixtures in the 2019/20 Championship-winning season?

1.
2.
3.
4.
5.

9. Can you name the Whites' first five goalscorers from the current Championship campaign?

1.
2.
3.
4.
5.

7. Can you identify the following players from their 2023/24 Leeds United squad numbers?

1. 5
2. 8
3. 22
4. 25
5. 28

10. Can you name the clubs the following players were signed or loaned from?

1. Ethan Ampadu
2. Joel Piroe
3. Glen Kamara
4. Joe Rodon
5. Jaidon Anthony

ANSWERS ON PAGE 62

SENSATIONAL STOPPERS

DAVID HARVEY, JOHN LUKIC AND NIGEL MARTYN WERE ALL GREAT LEEDS 'KEEPERS. CONTINUING THAT PROUD TRADITION IS CURRENT WHITES STOPPER ILLAN MESLIER.

David Harvey enjoyed just shy of 20 years as a Leeds United goalkeeper and was part of some of the best times in the club's history.

He was present for much of Leeds' success in the 1970s, winning an FA Cup in 1972, a league title in 1974 and a handful of European honours too.

He was quick off his line, willing to claim crosses and capable of great saves. He received praise for standing up tall in the big moments, but also keeping things calm and composed at the back for himself and others.

DAVID HARVEY

DATE OF BIRTH: February 7, 1948

PLACE OF BIRTH: Leeds

NATIONALITY: English

LEEDS UNITED APPEARANCES: 447

LEEDS UNITED CLEAN SHEETS: 152

LEEDS UNITED DEBUT: October 13, 1965
Leeds United 2-4 West Bromwich Albion (League Cup)

John Lukic took over from David Harvey between the sticks in 1979, ensuring a fine lineage of goalkeepers at Elland Road that spanned decades.

He took in two separate spells at the club, leaving in 1983 for Arsenal after Leeds dropped into the Second Division, but returning in 1990 with the club on the up and ready to compete for silverware again. Two years later, the Whites won the final First Division title before it was renamed as the Premier League.

A towering figure, Lukic dominated in the air, but also boasted fine reflexes too.

JOHN LUKIC

DATE OF BIRTH: December 11, 1960

PLACE OF BIRTH: Chesterfield

NATIONALITY: English

LEEDS UNITED APPEARANCES: 431

LEEDS UNITED CLEAN SHEETS: 150

LEEDS UNITED DEBUT: October 3, 1979
Leeds United 3-0 Valetta (UEFA Cup)

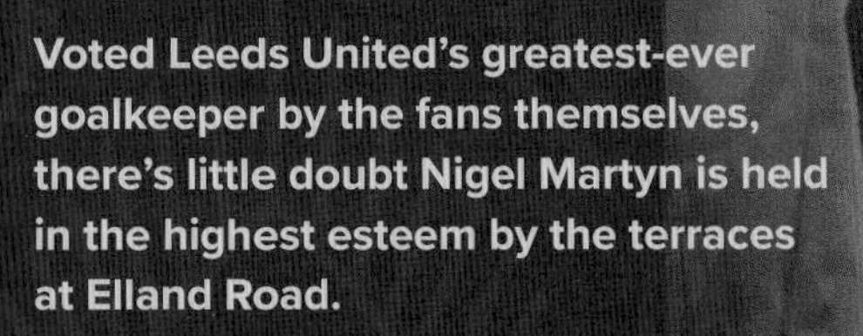

Voted Leeds United's greatest-ever goalkeeper by the fans themselves, there's little doubt Nigel Martyn is held in the highest esteem by the terraces at Elland Road.

He was a rock between the sticks in a excellent Premier League Leeds side, playing a huge part in a string of consistent top-five finishes and a magical run to the Champions League semi-finals in 2001.

His reflexes were great and he commanded his box well, but his best trait was perhaps his agility, the way he scurried across his line to make incredible point-blank saves never ceased to amaze.

NIGEL MARTYN

DATE OF BIRTH: August 11, 1966

PLACE OF BIRTH: St Austell

NATIONALITY: English

LEEDS UNITED APPEARANCES: 273

LEEDS UNITED CLEAN SHEETS: 105

LEEDS UNITED DEBUT: August 17, 1996
Derby County 3-3 Leeds (Premier League)

ILLAN MESLIER

DATE OF BIRTH: March 2, 2000

PLACE OF BIRTH: Lorient, France

NATIONALITY: French

LEEDS UNITED APPEARANCES: 126*

LEEDS UNITED CLEAN SHEETS: 30*

LEEDS UNITED DEBUT: January 6, 2020
Arsenal 1-0 Leeds United (FA Cup)

*AS AT THE END OF THE 2022/23 SEASON

It's not often you see goalkeepers command regular first-team football aged 20, but Illan Meslier's modern style catapulted him ahead of his peers in 2020 and he has not looked back since.

Then-manager Marcelo Bielsa identified two key traits in the Frenchman's game: His confident distribution from the back and his excellence in one v one scenarios. Both were called upon frequently as Leeds' high-risk, high-reward style saw them promoted into the Premier League and then finish in the top half.

During this time he carved out a deserved reputation as one of Europe's brightest young goalkeeping prospects.

ANSWERS

PAGE 29: FOOTY PHRASES

Keepie Uppie.

PAGE 34: A-Z QUIZ

A. Austrian. B. Burnley. C. Crystal Palace. D. Derby County. E. Egyptian. F. France. G. Goodison Park (Everton). H. Huddersfield Town. I. Iran. J. Jamaica. K. Kenilworth Road. L. Ladapo, Freddie. M. Middlesbrough (Chuba Akpom). N. Norwegian. O. Oldham Athletic. P. Pukki, Teemu. Q. Qatar. R. Real Madrid. S. Southampton. T. Toffolo, Harry. U. Undav, Deniz. V. Vardy, Jamie. W. Wilson, Ben (Coventry City). X. Xavier, Abel. Y. Yeovil Town. Z. Zenden, Boudewijn.

PAGE 42: FAN'TASTIC

PAGE 45: WHICH BALL

Top: E. Bottom. D.

PAGE 47: SPOT THE DIFFERENCE

PAGE 48: BEHIND THE BADGE

A. Sam Byram. B. Joe Gelhardt. C. Pascal Struck. D. Luke Ayling. E. Crysencio Summerville. F. Ethan Ampadu. G. Archie Gray. H. Ian Poveda.

PAGE 58: HIGH FIVES

QUIZ 1:

1. 2022/23, Rodrigo (13 goals). 2. 2021/22, Raphina (11 goals). 3. 2020/21, Patrick Bamford (17 goals). 4. 2019/20, Patrick Bamford (16 goals). 5. 2018/19, Kemar Roofe (14 goals).

QUIZ 2:

1. 2022/23, Fulham (fifth round). 2. 2022/23, Accrington Stanley (fourth round). 3. 2022/23, Cardiff City (third round). 4. 2021/22 West Ham United (third round). 5. 2020/21 Crawley Town (third round).

QUIZ 3:

1. Sam Allardyce. 2. Javi Gracia. 3. Jesse Marsch. 4. Marcelo Bielsa. 5. Paul Heckingbottom.

QUIZ 4:

1. Wolverhampton Wanderers (2022/23). 2. Barnsley (2022/23). 3. Arsenal (2021/22). 4. Fulham (2021/22). 5. Crewe Alexandra (2021/22).

QUIZ 5:

1. Championship champions (2019/20). 2. First Division champions (1991/92. 3. Second Division champions (1989/90). 4. First Division champions (1973/74. 5. FA Cup winners (1971/72).

QUIZ 6:

1. Ben White (46 Championship starts).
2. Stuart Dallas, Jack Harrison & Mateusz Klich (45 Championship starts).
3. Patrick Bamford (43 Championship starts).
4. Kalvin Phillips (37 Championship starts).
5. Liam Cooper and Casilla (36 Championship starts).

QUIZ 7:

1. Charlie Cresswell (No.5). 2. Glen Kamara (No.8). 3. Archie Gray (No.22). 4. Sam Bryam (No.25). 5. Karl Darlow (No.28).

QUIZ 8:

1. 2009/10, Manchester United 0-1 Leeds United (FA Cup).
2. 2002/03, Leeds United 1-0 Manchester United (Premier League).
3. 1997/98, Leeds United 1-0 Manchester United (Premier League).
4. 1995/96, Leeds United 3-1 Manchester United (Premier League).
5. 1994/95, Leeds United 2-1 Manchester United (Premier League).

QUIZ 9:

1. Liam Cooper (v Cardiff City). 2. Crysencio Summerville (v Cardiff City). 3. Luke Ayling (v West Bromwich Albion). 4. Georginio Rutter (v Ipswich Town). 5. Wilfried Gnonto (v Ipswich Town).

QUIZ 10:

1. Chelsea. 2. Swansea City. 3. Glasgow Rangers. 4. Tottenham Hotspur. 5. AFC Bournemouth.